LET'S MAKE MAGIC

Jon Day

Illustrated by
Chris Fisher

Contents

Easy Magic

Kingfisher Books

NEW YORK

All about easy magic

This section shows you how to do eleven great tricks with everyday objects - matches, bits of string, empty bottles, and other things you should be able to find easily at home. On these two pages you can discover some tips and hints to help you become a successful magician.

Practice in front of a mirror to get an audience's eye view.

Hints

1 Make sure you have all the equipment ready and in the right place before you start to do a trick.

2 Resist the temptation to tell your friends how a trick works – even if they are begging you to tell them! Keep them guessing, and that way they will be even more impressed with your skill.

3 Never perform the same trick more than once. That makes it too easy for your friends to work out how it was done.

Safety warning:
Be sensible when doing tricks involving matches. Use only spent matches, that have already been burned. Keep all matches and matchboxes away from younger children.

Write yourself a performing script – and learn it by heart. You could record it on tape and listen to it over and over again until you get it rig[ht]

The tricks in this section are called easy because they all involve easily found objects, and they are all quite simple to understand. But don't forget that even the simplest trick can astound people if you perform it smoothly and confidently!

Magicians know that there are two things needed to make good magic. The first is **practice.** Work at each trick until you can do it easily and with confidence. That accounts for about ten percent of a magician's success.

Ninety percent of a magician's success comes from the way the trick is done – the **presentation.** That means knowing how to act, what to say, and how to persuade people to see only what you want them to see. That's the really tricky bit!

Flyaway money

Things you need

Large sheet of white paper

Sheet of colored paper

Piece of white paper to fit top of glass

Coin

Pencil

Glass

Glue

Make a coin appear and disappear under an upturned glass.

Get ready . . .

Make a paper lid and a cover for the glass.

1 Put the upturned glass on the smaller piece of white paper and draw around the top with a pencil

2 Cut out the circle and stick it to the top of the glass with glue. Trim it so it fits exactly.

3 Cut a strip of colored paper the same height as the glass. Bend it around the glass.

Make sure the cover slips on and off the glass easily.

4 Stick the edges together to make a cover for the glass. Make sure it slips on and off it easily.

5 Spread the large white sheet of paper on the table where you are going to perform.

4

Trick time

1 Put the upturned glass, the colored paper cover and the coin on the large sheet of white paper.

2 Put the colored paper cover over the glass.

3 Pick up the cover and the glass together and place them over the coin.

4 Lift off the paper cover – and the coin has vanished!

5 To make the coin reappear, reverse the process. Put the cover over the glass and lift both to one side. There's the coin! Now remove the cover.

Don't let anyone see the paper lid on the glass!

Snap!

Things you need

Handkerchief with a deep hem

Two matchsticks

Break a matchstick in two – and then make it whole again.

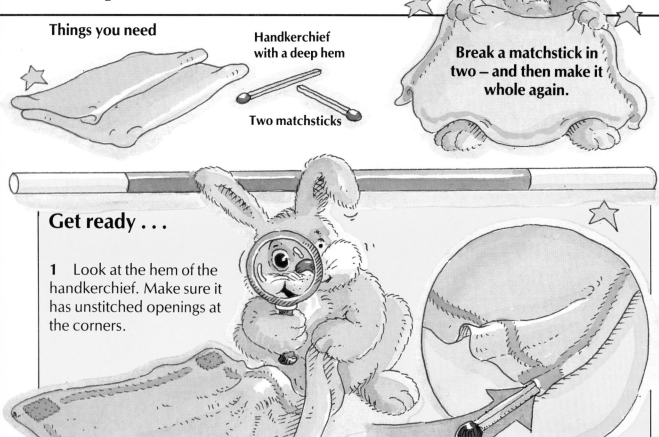

Get ready . . .

1 Look at the hem of the handkerchief. Make sure it has unstitched openings at the corners.

2 Put one of the matches into the hem, using one of the corner openings. Feed it along so it is some way from the corner.

Trick time

1 Put the handkerchief on the table, making sure the corner containing the match is nearest to you.

2 Put the other match on the center of the handkerchief.

6

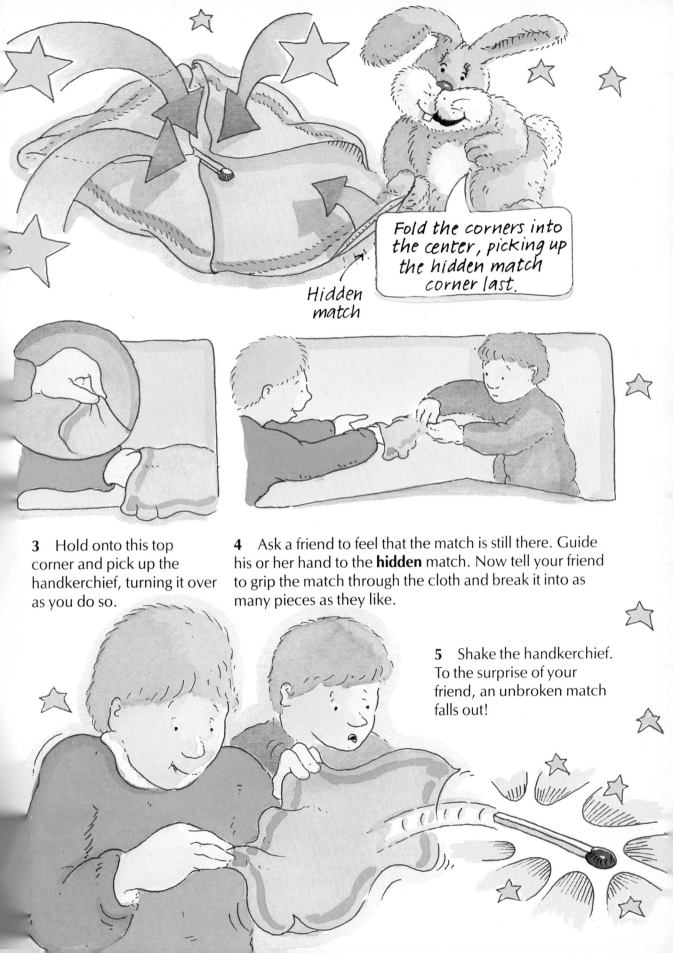

Fold the corners into the center, picking up the hidden match corner last.

Hidden match

3 Hold onto this top corner and pick up the handkerchief, turning it over as you do so.

4 Ask a friend to feel that the match is still there. Guide his or her hand to the **hidden** match. Now tell your friend to grip the match through the cloth and break it into as many pieces as they like.

5 Shake the handkerchief. To the surprise of your friend, an unbroken match falls out!

Mint on a string

Things you need

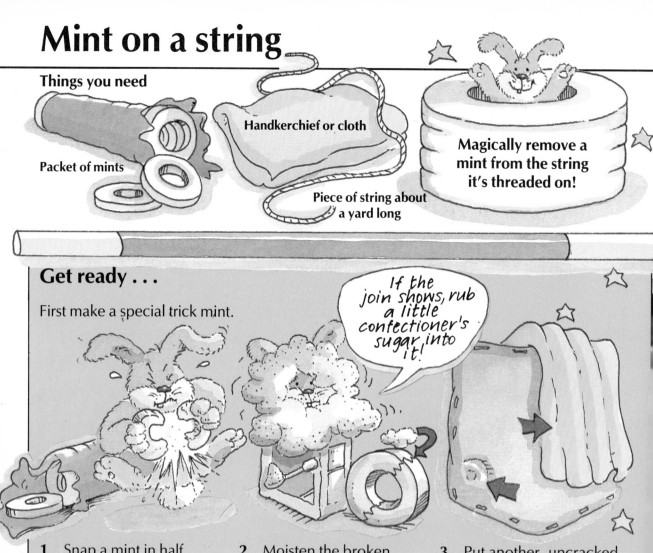

Packet of mints

Handkerchief or cloth

Piece of string about a yard long

Magically remove a mint from the string it's threaded on!

Get ready . . .

First make a special trick mint.

If the join shows, rub a little confectioner's sugar into it!

1 Snap a mint in half, making sure you get a nice clean break.

2 Moisten the broken edges and stick them back together. Put the mint back in the packet.

3 Put another, uncracked, mint in your right-hand pocket, along with a cloth or large handkerchief.

Trick time

Give them the string and ask them to thread the mint onto it.

1 Take the special mint out of the packet and give it to someone in the audience.

The mint breaks silently because it's been broken before!

2 Take the cloth and the uncracked mint out of your pocket. Keep this mint hidden in your right hand.

3 Drape the cloth over the mint on the string. Put both hands under the cloth, snap the trick mint and hide the pieces in your left hand.

4 Hold the unbroken mint against the string with your right hand. Remove the cloth and broken mint with your left hand and put them in your left pocket.

5 Appear to pluck the whole mint off the string and hand it to the audience to examine.

Now how did she do that?

The magic bottle

Things you need

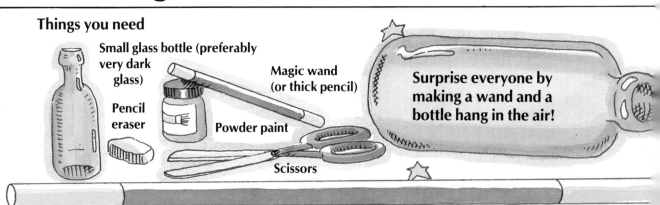

Small glass bottle (preferably very dark glass)

Pencil eraser

Magic wand (or thick pencil)

Powder paint

Scissors

Surprise everyone by making a wand and a bottle hang in the air!

Get ready . . .

1 The bottle must be dark so nobody can see into it. If yours isn't, you can paint it on the inside.

2 To paint the bottle, mix up some powder paint and pour it inside. Put the lid back on and shake it about 50 times. Remove the lid and pour out the paint.

3 You can make a wand out of wooden doweling or a very large pencil.

4 Cut a piece of rubber from the eraser. It must be about as big as a pea – just the right size to wedge itself between the bottle neck and the wand.

Trick time

Rubber in here.

1 Put the wand and the bottle on the table. Hide the bit of rubber in your hand.

2 Pass the bottle to someone and ask them to make sure it's empty.

3 Take back the bottle. Give your friend the wand to examine, meanwhile slipping the bit of rubber into the bottle.

4 Put the bottle on the table, take the wand back and drop it into the bottle.

Rubber piece

Make sure the rubber piece gets wedged between the wand and the neck of the bottle.

5 Pick up the bottle and wand like this. and **very slowly** turn them upside down.

6 Leg go of the wand. It's amazing - it doesn't fall!

Hide the rubber piece in your pocket!

7 Holding the wand and the bottle, slowly turn them upright again. Let the bottle go - and it doesn't fall!

8 Give the wand a little push to release the rubber. Take the wand out and give it to someone to examine.

9 While, they're looking at the wand, tip the bottle up and remove the rubber. Now give your friends the bottle to examine. Ask them to try the trick - and bet they can't do it!

11

The vanishing key

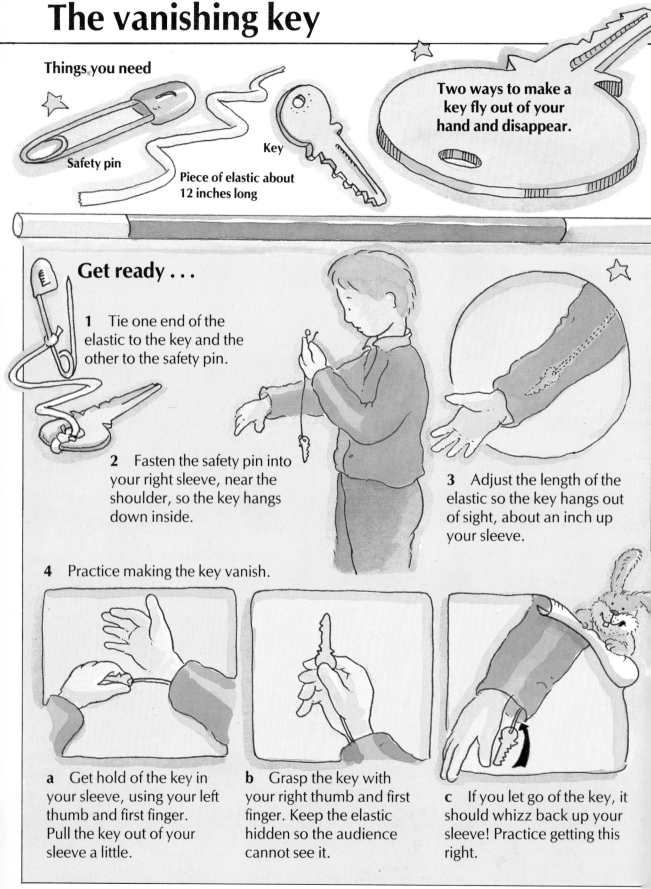

Things you need

Safety pin

Key

Piece of elastic about 12 inches long

Two ways to make a key fly out of your hand and disappear.

Get ready . . .

1 Tie one end of the elastic to the key and the other to the safety pin.

2 Fasten the safety pin into your right sleeve, near the shoulder, so the key hangs down inside.

3 Adjust the length of the elastic so the key hangs out of sight, about an inch up your sleeve.

4 Practice making the key vanish.

a Get hold of the key in your sleeve, using your left thumb and first finger. Pull the key out of your sleeve a little.

b Grasp the key with your right thumb and first finger. Keep the elastic hidden so the audience cannot see it.

c If you let go of the key, it should whizz back up your sleeve! Practice getting this right.

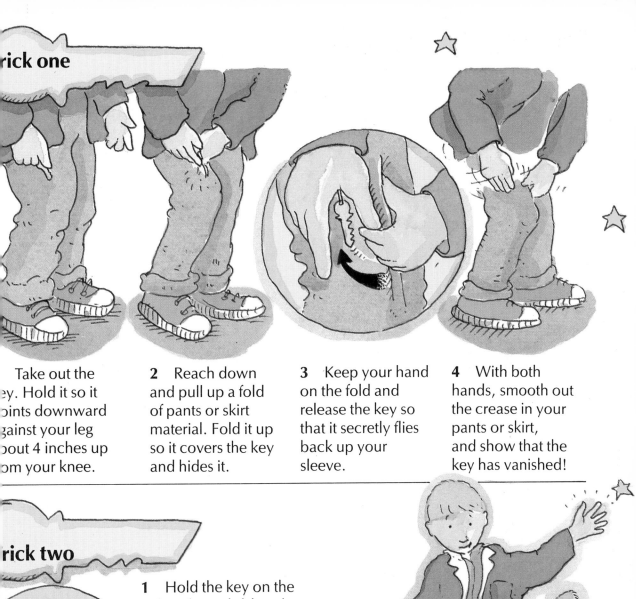

Trick one

1 Take out the key. Hold it so it points downward against your leg about 4 inches up from your knee.

2 Reach down and pull up a fold of pants or skirt material. Fold it up so it covers the key and hides it.

3 Keep your hand on the fold and release the key so that it secretly flies back up your sleeve.

4 With both hands, smooth out the crease in your pants or skirt, and show that the key has vanished!

Trick two

1 Hold the key on the palm of your left hand.

2 Pretend to take it in your left hand, making a fist, but actually release it and let it fly back up your sleeve.

3 Show your empty right hand – then slowly open your left hand. The key has vanished!

13

The floating pencil

Things you need

Pencil

Blob of adhesive putty

Small glass bottle

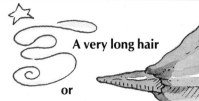

A very long hair

or

about 20 inches of nylon "invisible" sewing thread or very fine nylon fishing line

Make a pencil mysteriously jump up and down inside a bottle

Get ready . . .

A very long human hair works best in this trick, but if you can't get one use a very fine "invisible" nylon thread.

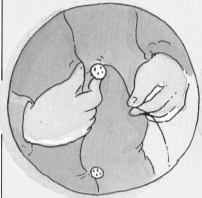

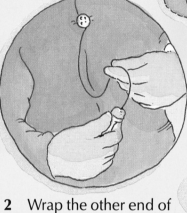

Stick the adhesive putty to the end of the pencil.

1 Tie one end of the hair to a button on your jacket, blouse, or shirt.

2 Wrap the other end of the hair around a small blob of adhesive putty and squash it in to fasten it securely.

Trick time

1 Hold the bottle in one hand. Drop the pencil in, adhesive putty end first.

2 If you move the bottle back and forth, the pencil rises and falls very mysteriously.

3 Do this a few times then push the bottle even further forward. Now the pencil "floats" out of the bottle.

4 Take the pencil in your free hand and reach out to offer it to the audience to examine.

5 As you stretch your arm, the adhesive putty comes off the bottom of the pencil and hangs out of sight, on the end of the hair.

I bet nobody will be able to work out what makes the pencil move!

Match me if you can!

Things you need

Two identical full boxes of matches

Make sure they have the same labels on both sides

Pencil

Scissors

Ask a friend to copy your actions exactly – but they will never do it correctly.

Get ready . . .

First, make a special trick matchbox.

Put the dot here.

1 Cut out **a little under one half** of the bottom of the tray of one matchbox.

2 Make a small pencil mark on the outside cover to mark the cut-out end.

3 Put the matches back in the tray and put the box back together.

Trick time

Make each move slowly so that your friend can copy you.

1 Ask a friend to sit opposite you. Take the trick matchbox (with the uncut side facing up). Give your friend the other box. Tell them to do exactly as you do.

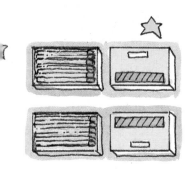
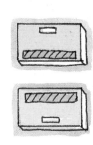

2   Keeping the box on the table, slide the tray out of the cover. Ask your friend to do the same.

3   Push the full tray back into the cover. Your friend must do the same.

4   Twist the box around one turn clockwise. Your friend does the same.

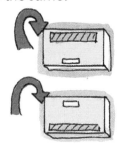
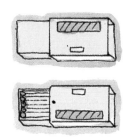

5   Turn the box over completely. Your friend does the same.

6   Open yours a little at the dotted end. Your friend's box will be the wrong way up!

7   Ask the friend to adjust his or her matchbox so it looks like yours.

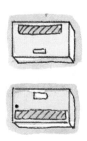
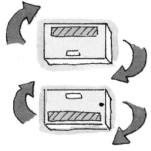

8   Close the boxes.

9   Twist them around one turn.

10   Turn them over completely.

11   Slide the tray out of your box - and your friend is wrong again!

This could go on all night- but your friend will always be wrong.

Spool Magic

Things you need

Two pieces of string each about a yard long

Thread Spool

Remove a thread spool from a piece of string without cutting the string.

Get ready . . .

It looks as if you're holding two separate pieces of string.

1 Fold the two pieces of string in half. Put one loop through the other, as in this drawing.

2 Hold the strings so that your fingers and thumb cover them where they are looped together.

Trick time

1 Holding the strings as shown above, pick up the thread spool and let two ends of the string drop into the hole in the spool. If the ends of the string aren't stiff enough to drop easily into the hole, bind them with tape before you start the trick.

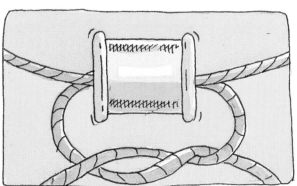

2 Gently feed the string through until the looped part is inside the spool.

As you pull, hide the looped part in your fingers.

3 Take the strings by the ends and hold them loosely, with the spool threaded on. **Don't pull the strings.**

4 Ask a friend to hold the strings and spool. Tell them to give you two strings – one from each side of the spool. Tie these two strings together in a knot.

5 Give the ends of the knotted string back to your friend and ask them to hold all the strings tightly. Cover the spool with your hand, gripping it firmly, and slide your hand back and forth until you feel the spool come free of the string.

6 Keep the spool covered by your hand. Carry on sliding your hand back and forward, then pull the strings slightly toward you and "pluck" the spool off the strings. Your friend will be very surprised!

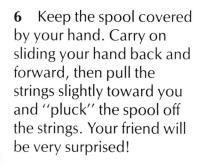

Magic bangle

Things you need

Two identical bangles or bracelets

Piece of string about a yard long

Jacket with inside pocket and wide sleeves

Make a bangle appear by magic on a piece of string tied between your wrists.

Get ready . . .

Put one of the bangles on your left arm and push it up your sleeve so it is hidden out of sight.

Hidden bangle

Trick time

1   Pass the bangle and the piece of string to a member of the audience. Ask them to examine both carefully.

2   Ask someone to tie the ends of the string to your wrists as firmly as they can.

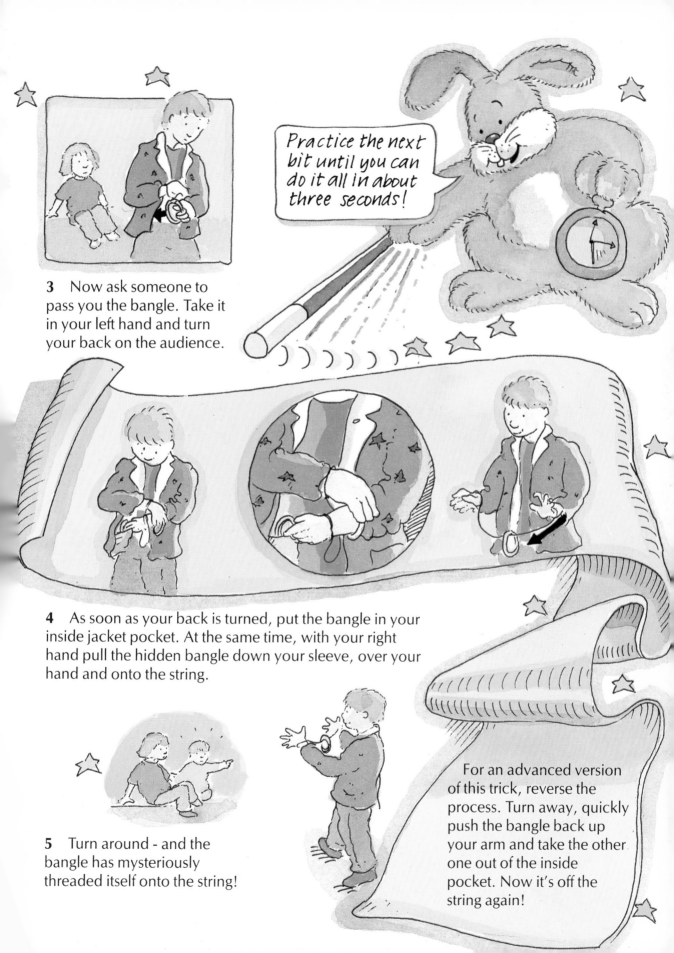

Practice the next bit until you can do it all in about three seconds!

3 Now ask someone to pass you the bangle. Take it in your left hand and turn your back on the audience.

4 As soon as your back is turned, put the bangle in your inside jacket pocket. At the same time, with your right hand pull the hidden bangle down your sleeve, over your hand and onto the string.

5 Turn around - and the bangle has mysteriously threaded itself onto the string!

For an advanced version of this trick, reverse the process. Turn away, quickly push the bangle back up your arm and take the other one out of the inside pocket. Now it's off the string again!

A knotty problem

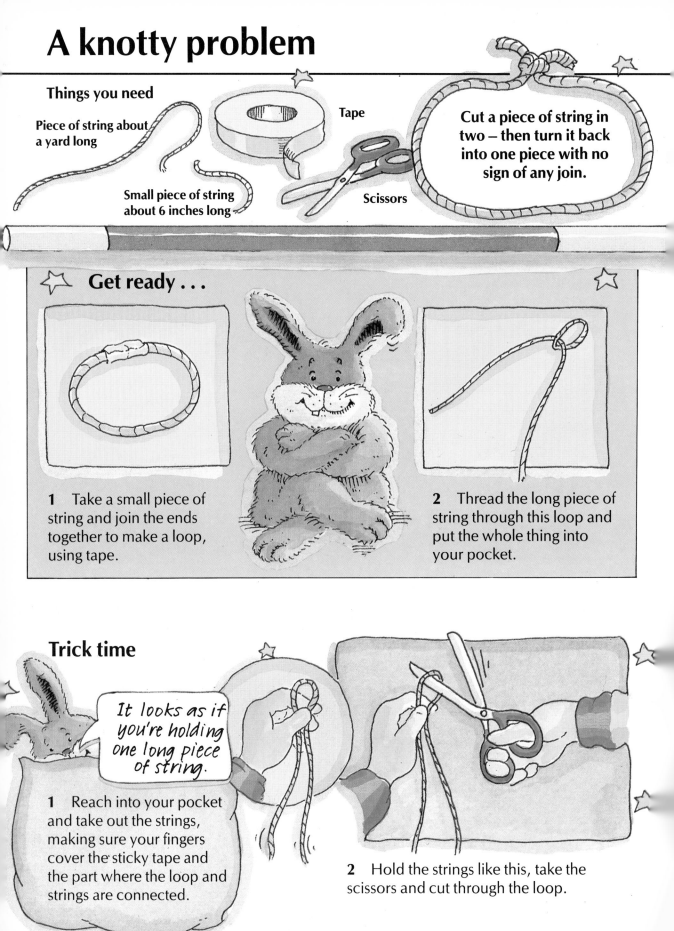

Things you need

Piece of string about a yard long

Small piece of string about 6 inches long

Tape

Scissors

Cut a piece of string in two – then turn it back into one piece with no sign of any join.

Get ready . . .

1 Take a small piece of string and join the ends together to make a loop, using tape.

2 Thread the long piece of string through this loop and put the whole thing into your pocket.

Trick time

It looks as if you're holding one long piece of string.

1 Reach into your pocket and take out the strings, making sure your fingers cover the sticky tape and the part where the loop and strings are connected.

2 Hold the strings like this, take the scissors and cut through the loop.

Knot these two ends together →

The short string is now knotted around the long string.

3 Put the scissors down and tie the cut ends in a knot. Keep the loop hidden by your fingers.

4 Show everyone the cut and knotted string. Then take one end of the string in your left hand and with your right hand begin to wind it around your fingers.

The loop is in here

5 As you wind it, the string goes through your right fist and you can secretly slip the knotted loop off it.

6 Put your right hand in your right pocket for your wand, dropping in the loop as you do so.

7 Wave the wand over your left hand; say some magic words, and begin to unwind the string from your hand.

8 Throw the string to your friends and let them examine it. There is no sign of a cut of a knot!.

23

Finger on the pulse

You will need

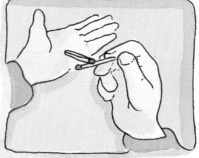

Two matches

Your fingernails are covered in tiny grooves. These grooves are the secret in this simple but surprising trick.

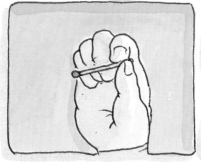

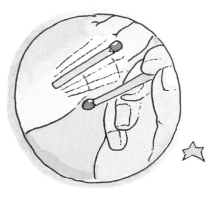

1 Hold a match firmly between your thumb and first finger. Press it down onto the nail of your second finger.

2 Put the second match on your left hand. Rest one end of it on the first match.

3 Press down hard on the first match so that it skids on the tiny grooves in your nail. This makes the second match jump.

Even when they are very close, your friends should not be able to see the first match move at all!

Ask a friend to hold your wrist while you do this trick. Tell them the match is jumping in time with their pulse.

Have fun with Card Magic next...

24

Card Magic

All about card magic

This section shows you how to do ten great card tricks. On this page you can find out about some of the things you will need to become a good magician.

You don't have to dress up, but wearing a **cloak** and **hat** is fun and may help you give a better performance.

Pockets are useful for hiding cards in.

You can make a **magic wand** out of wooden doweling. Paint it black and white.

You need a **table** to do many of the tricks on. Cover it with a **cloth** so the cards do not slide about while you are performing.

The most important thing you need to be a good magician is **practice.**

Try out the tricks in private, doing them again and again until you can do them smoothly.

Try out tricks in front of a mirror to get an audience's eye view.

Some tricks require tape, scissors, pencils, etc. There is a list of these things at the beginning of each trick.

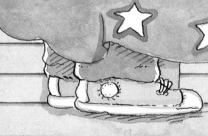

Some special card words are explained in full on page 48.

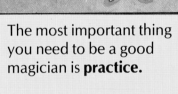

You need two identical decks of playing cards. One is your **performing deck.** The other is a **spare deck** which you use to make special trick cards.

If you have difficulty holding full-size cards, you can buy small-size decks.

Use all your **acting ability.** You have to persuade people that what they are seeing is magic! Knowing what to say, and how to say it, is as important as knowing how a trick works.

Hints

1 At the beginning of each trick, make sure you have all the equipment ready and in the right place.

2 Never repeat a trick straight away, even when people beg you to do so. They will know just what to look for, and so may guess the secret of the trick.

3 Never show anyone how you did a trick. That is your secret as a magician!

Aces high

Things you need

Deck of cards

Get a friend to find all four Aces without trying

Get ready . . .

Place the four Aces face down on top of the deck, but don't let anyone see you doing it.

Trick time

1 Tell a friend that he or she is going to do all the magic by finding the four Aces without even looking at the cards!

2 Ask them to pick up the deck and divide it into four piles of about the same size. **Make sure the pile with the Aces on top is in fourth place.**

This is the the pile with the Aces on top.

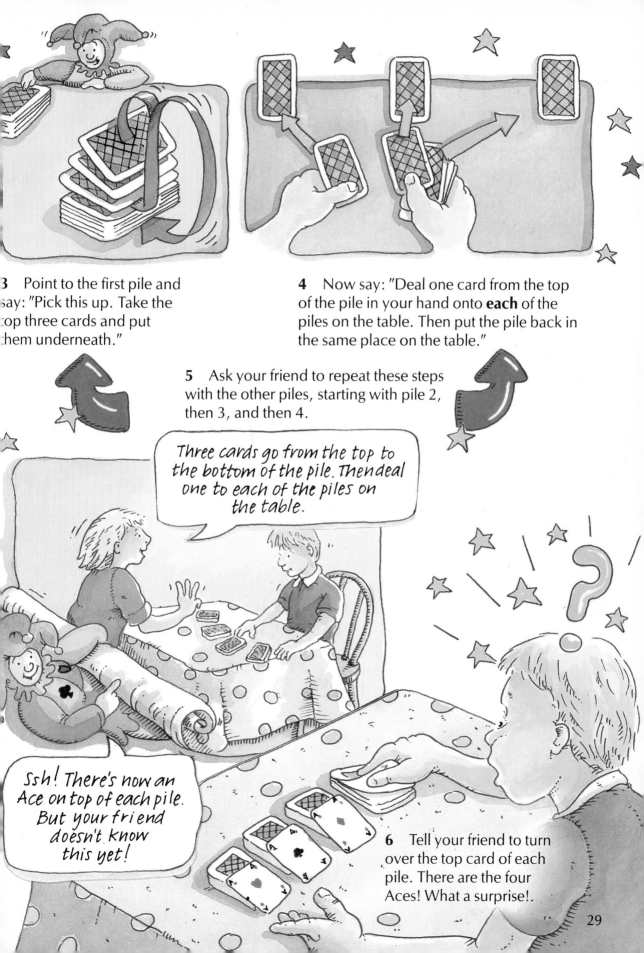

3 Point to the first pile and say: "Pick this up. Take the top three cards and put them underneath."

4 Now say: "Deal one card from the top of the pile in your hand onto **each** of the piles on the table. Then put the pile back in the same place on the table."

5 Ask your friend to repeat these steps with the other piles, starting with pile 2, then 3, and then 4.

Three cards go from the top to the bottom of the pile. Then deal one to each of the piles on the table.

Ssh! There's now an Ace on top of each pile. But your friend doesn't know this yet!

6 Tell your friend to turn over the top card of each pile. There are the four Aces! What a surprise!.

29

The whispering cards

Astonish your friends by getting cards to talk to you!

Things you need

Deck of cards

Pencil

Twelve identical envelopes

Get ready . . .

1 Take four of the envelopes and mark each one with a tiny pencil dot in the top **left**-hand corner of flap.

2 Take another four and mark them with a dot in the top **right**-hand corner.

3 Leave the other four envelopes blank.

4 Stack all the envelopes in a pile in this order.

Left-dotted on top
Right-dotted in the middle.
Blank underneath.

Trick time

1 Tell everyone that you can hear cards talking! You will be able to say whether a card is a Jack, Queen, or King just by listening to it whispering to you!

2 Take the four Jacks, four Queens, and four Kings from the deck. Put them in a pile with Jacks on top, then Queens, then Kings.

There's no need to seal the envelopes, but turn them over so nobody can see the dots.

3 Put a Jack in each of the top four envelopes, a Queen in the next four, and a King in the last four.

4 Give the envelopes to someone and ask them to mix them up on the table.

Left-hand dot = Jack

Right-hand dot = Queen

No dot = King

I can hear a young man's voice. He says his name is Jack!

5 Now pick one envelope from the table. Hold it up, looking casually for a dot on the back as you do so.

I can hear a woman's voice. It must be the Queen!

This one is a man's voice! It's the King!

6 Now you begin acting! Hold the envelope to your ear and listen to it, as if you could hear a whisper inside. Say: "Tell me who you are please." Tell your audience if it is a King, Queen, or Jack inside. Make up your own script, or follow the one used here. Take out the card to see if you are right. (Of course you are!)

7 Repeat steps **5** and **6** with each of the envelopes. Everyone will be amazed!

Jumping Jack

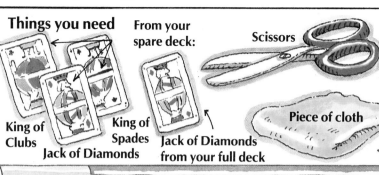

Things you need

From your spare deck:

King of Clubs

King of Spades

Jack of Diamonds

Jack of Diamonds from your full deck

Scissors

Piece of cloth

Make the Jack jump out of your friend's hands and into your pocket!

Get ready . . .

Trim off ¹⁄₁₆ in.

¾ in.

1 Cut a piece about this size out of one end of the spare Jack.

2 Make the two Kings slightly narrower by trimming off about ¹⁄₁₆ inch from one edge of each.

3 Put the "real" Jack of Diamonds in your pocket.

Trick time

You need to be seated at a table to do this trick.

Cut part hidden behind King.

Make sure the cut end is between their thumb and forefinger.

1 Hold the three cards like this, and show them to your friends.

2 Tell your friends you will make the Jack jump out of their hands into your pocket.

3 Close the cards and ask someone to hold them between their thumb and first finger.

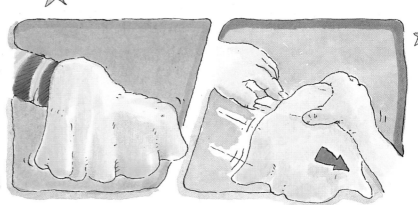

4 Say: "In a minute this is what I'll do to make the Jack jump. I'll just show you."

5 Drape the cloth over your friend's hand and quickly remove it again, **taking the Jack with you.** Do this by gripping the edges of the card and pulling. Only the Jack will move, and your friend will feel nothing.

6 You have already done the trick, but nobody realizes! Drop the cloth and Jack into your lap.

7 Say: "Now I'm going to put the cloth over your hand and make the Jack jump out into my pocket."

8 Put the cloth over your friend's hand and "steal" the Jack again.

9 Ask your friend to look for the Jack. It has gone!

10 Pull the (other) Jack from your pocket . . . proving it jumped as you said it would do!

The impossible card trick

Things you need

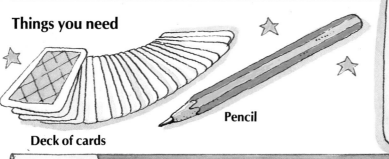

Pencil

Deck of cards

Find the card your friend chose without looking at the deck at all!

Get ready . . .

1 Choose any card and mark it lightly with pencil dots in the top-left and bottom-right corners.

2 Put your **key card** back into the deck **in the 26th position from the top.**

*This is called a **key card**. It will help you find any card your friend chooses.*

Pencil dot

26th card

Pencil dot

25 cards

Key card is number 26

Trick time

*This pile **must** be more than half the pack or the trick won't work.*

Pile A

Pile B

Pile C

Your key card will now be in pile B.

1 Place the deck face down on the table (pile A).

2 Get a friend to lift off more than half the cards and place them on the right (pile B).

3 Now ask your friend to lift off "about half" of pile B and put these cards on the right, making pile C.

34

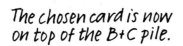
The chosen card is now on top of the B+C pile.

Point out that so far you have not touched the cards at all.

4 Point to pile C and say: "Pick this pile up and shuffle it. Look at the top card, remember it, and then put it back on top."

5 Then say: "Now put the cards (pile C) on top of this pile (pile B)."

6 Ask your friend to pick up pile A, shuffle it and put it on top of the B + C pile.

Make sure you can see the top left-hand corner of every card.

If this is card 1...

...then this is card 26.

If you get to the end of the row before reaching number 26, go back to the left-hand end and carry on counting.

7 Pick up the cards and spread them out on a cloth-covered table or carpet. Spread them from left to right, making them overlap.

8 Ask your friend to hold your wrist, so you can feel his or her vibrations! Move your finger over the cards, from left to right. When you see the pencil dot on the **key card,** count it (silently!) as 1. Carry on counting until you reach card 26, **which is your friend's chosen card.**

But that's impossible isn't it?

9 Don't pick the card out right away. Hover around it for a while, picking up the vibrations!

10 Pull out the card, still face down. Turn it over . . . **it's the card your friend chose!**

Circus trick

Things you need

Deck of cards

Your friends will be so sure you've made a mistake they'll bet their money on it.

Get ready . . .

This simple trick was once used by circus and fairground entertainers to cheat people out of their money.

With practice, you will find it an easy trick to do. But don't take your friend's money - you're a magician, not a cheat!

Trick time

1 Ask a friend to shuffle the cards. As you take them back, sneak a look at the bottom card. Make sure you remember it - it's called the **key card.**

2 Spread the cards out between your hands. Ask your friend who shuffled to choose a card and remember what it is.

This is the key card.

Chosen card

Chosen card

Chosen card

Key card and chosen card

3 Gather the cards back together. Tell your friend to put their chosen card back on top of the deck.

4 Now cut the deck (see page 48 to find out how to do this). Your friend's card will move to the middle of the pack - and the **key card** will be on top of it!

5 Hold the deck face down. Deal one card at a time, face up, in a line across the table.

Tell everyone you'll be able to pick out the chosen card just by feeling it. Pretend to feel each card carefully as you deal it out onto the table.

6 When you deal out the key card, **the next card you turn over will be the one your friend chose.**

Keep a straight face.

Chosen card

7 Deal out the chosen card, feeling it as before. Play-act a bit, taking your time and looking unsure.

8 Pretend to reject the card, then deal out three or four more. Look exicted about the next card. Keep it in your hand and say: "I bet the next card I turn over will be the one you chose."

Ha Ha! The card I chose is already on the table.

9 It's clear the chosen card is already on the table. Your friend will be happy to take on the bet.

10 Everyone expects you to turn over the card in your hand, but you reach out to the chosen card **on the table** and turn it over!

You've done just what you said you'd do, and your friend has lost the bet.

The vanishing Queen

Things you need

Scissors

From your spare deck:

A Queen   Two Aces   A Joker

Tape

Get ready . . .

1 Cut out the center section of the Queen card, keeping the head pieces from each end.

Cut out the center bit (about one third of the card).

Make sure the tape doesn't show on the other side.

2 Put the head pieces together, one facing up and one facing down. Join them together as shown, making a hinge with tape.

3 Fold up the hinged card, so the tape is inside. Slide it over one end of the Joker. Now you are ready to begin.

Trick time

1 Place the trick card between two Aces. Hold them in one hand. Show them to your audience.

Practice this bit to get it right.

2 Close the cards by pushing them down with your finger.

Hinged piece this end

3 Hold the cards face down. **Make sure the hinged edge is nearest to you.**

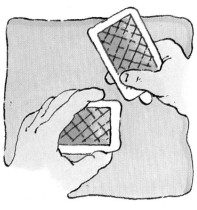

4 Pull out the bottom card and carefully place it face down on the table.

5 Put the next card (the Joker) down on the table. **Keep the hinged piece in your hand.**

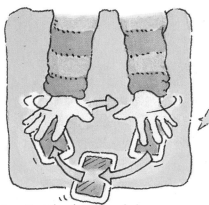

6 Put the last card down. Move the cards about, asking everyone to watch the Queen.

Slip the hinged piece into your pocket now, while nobody's looking!

7 Ask someone to point to the card they think is the Queen. Turn the other two cards over slowly.

8 Now turn over the last card. Everyone thinks it's the Queen, but it's the Joker! She has vanished!

Oops!

Things you need

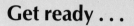

From your spare deck: Queen of Spades
King of Hearts   Any other card

Glue

Deck of cards

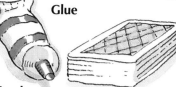

Oops - your friends
will think you've
chosen the wrong card!
But with a wave of
your hand you change
it to the right one.

Get ready . . .

Use the three spare cards to
make a trick "flap" card.

Glue

Glue

Fold the flap
up, and the card
is a King. Fold it
down, and it's a
Queen.

1 Fold the King and
Queen carefully in half.

2 Glue two halves
together, back to back.

3 Glue the other two
halves to the **face** of the
third card.

Flap card

Real Queen
of Spades

Now you're going
to ask a friend
to choose a card—
but you have
to make sure
it's the Queen
of Spades.

4 Put the flap card on the bottom of
your full deck. Make sure it shows the
King. Take the **real** King of Hearts out
of the deck. Place the **real** Queen of
Spades on top of the deck.

Trick time

This is the real Queen of Spades

1 Get a friend to cut the deck in half. Pick up the **bottom** half and rest it on the top half, like this.

2 Now distract your friend by talking! Say: "You could have cut the cards anywhere, couldn't you?"

3 Point to the cards and say: "And we've marked where you cut it like this." Pick up the pile resting on top.

Queen of Spades

Of course, it is the Queen of Spades – the card that was on top of the deck in the first place!

4 Point to the card on top of the other pile. Say: "Look at the card you cut to, and remember it."

5 Put the deck back together and ask your friend to put the chosen card into the middle.

7 Try this script:

You: Is this the card you chose?
Friend: No.
You: Oops! Sorry. What was it?
Friend: The Queen of Spades.
You: Then watch!

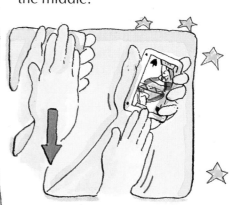

6 Shuffle the cards and look at them, face up. Find the King of Hearts flap card and hold it up.

8 Cover the King with your hand. "Wipe" your hand over it, pulling the flap down. Suddenly the Queen appears!

Hypnotized cards

Things you need

Deck of cards

Make lots of cards hang suspended in the air, as if by magic!

From your spare deck:
Any two cards

Scissors

Glue

Get ready . . .

1 Carefully cut a small flap in the center of one card, as shown here.

2 Put glue on the face of the cut card and stick it to the back of the other.

You must be able to move the flap up and down.

Make the sides of the flaps about half an inch long.

Be careful! Don't get glue on the flap area!

Fold the flap up along the dotted line.

3 When the glue is dry, place your trick flap card on the bottom of a deck of cards.

Put the flap card here. Make sure the flap is closed.

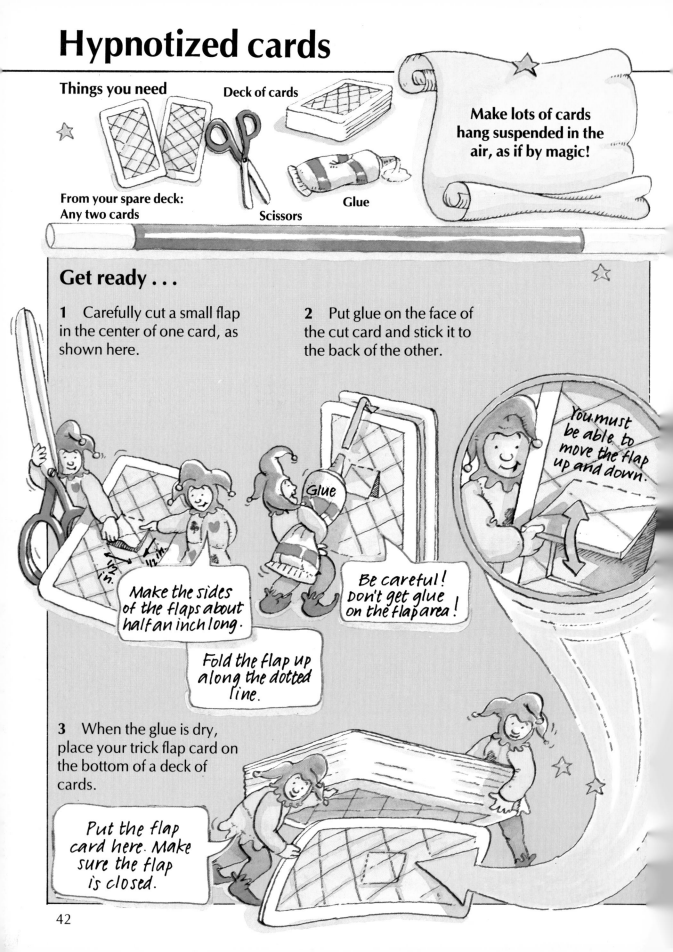

Trick time

1 Pick up the deck and slide off the flap card, secretly opening the flap as you do so.

2 Put the card face up on your hand so the flap goes between your second and third fingers.

3 Grip the flap to hold the card steady. Then start slowly sliding cards into the gap between your palm and the flap card.

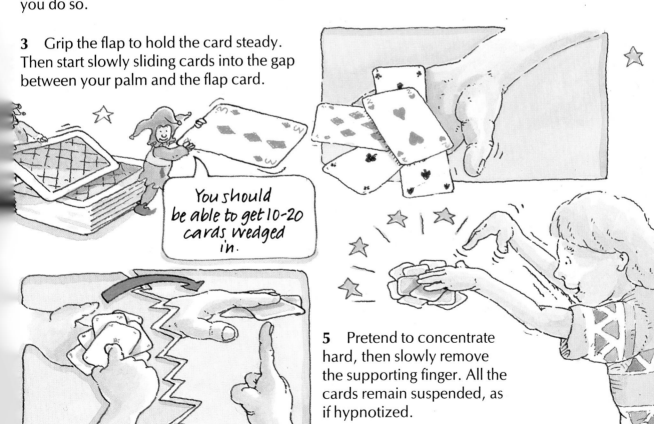

4 Press the first finger of your other hand on the cards to hold them steady. **Turn both hands over.**

5 Pretend to concentrate hard, then slowly remove the supporting finger. All the cards remain suspended, as if hypnotized.

6 After about 10 seconds, turn your hand over and let the cards fall onto the table. The flap will close and nobody will know how you did the trick.

43

The rising card

Things you need

Deck of cards

From your spare deck: Any four cards

Scissors

About 4 inches of elastic thread (shirring elastic)

or

a thin rubber band   Glue

Make any card your friend chooses rise slowly out of the pack!

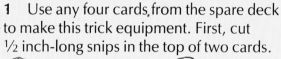

Get ready . . .

1 Use any four cards from the spare deck to make this trick equipment. First, cut ½ inch-long snips in the top of two cards.

2 Cut a piece of elastic thread about 4 inches long. Tie a knot near each end.

> The knots should be about 3 inches apart when the elastic isn't stretched.

The best elastic for this trick is shirring elastic - the kind used on party hats and masks. If you can't find any, you could cut open a thin rubber band and use it instead.

Glue here

Knot   *Knot*

3 Slip the elastic through the slits in the cards, with the knots at the back.

4 Glue the two other cards on so they cover the knots. Make sure all the cards are facing the same way.

Trick time

1 Pull the trick cards under the full deck, **with the elastic loop end toward you so you can see it.**

Knots

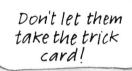
Don't let them take the trick card!

2 Spread the cards out face down between your hands and ask someone to choose one card.

3 Ask them to take the card, remember it, and put it face down on the table.

Page 48 shows how to cut a deck of cards.

4 Cut the deck so the bottom half moves to the top and the trick cards move to the middle.

Put card in here.

5 Pick up the chosen card and put it back into the deck, **into the elastic loop between the trick cards.**

Push it in to the loop.

6 Push the card in gently, making sure it goes into the loop and takes up the slack.

7 Grip the deck firmly and hold it up. Ask your friend to name the card they chose. **Gently** relax your grip. Their card will slowly rise from the deck like magic.

The knockout card trick

Things you need

A deck of cards

Pen

Small piece of paper

Guess what card your friend chose and find its name inside your shoe!

Get ready . . .

1 Write this message on the paper.

2 Fold it up and put it in your right shoe.

You are thinking of the 8 of Hearts

Put this message inside your shoe!

3 Find the 8 of Hearts and put it face down on top of the deck.

Now you must force your friend to choose the 8 of Hearts.

46

Trick time

Put the 8 of Hearts in here.

The 8 of Hearts stays between your hands.

1 Hold the deck behind your back, saying you can do this trick without looking.

2 Slip the 8 of Hearts off the deck and onto the back of your hand. Cover it with the other hand.

3 Turn your back on your friend. Ask them to take the deck, shuffle it, and put it back in your hands.

This step needs practice.

4 Turn to face your friend, sliding the 8 of Hearts back on top as you do so. Ask him or her to look at the top card, remember it, and put it back anywhere in the deck.

5 Look through the cards, trying to find the chosen one. Take out any card (except the 8 of Hearts). Without showing it, put it face down under your right foot.

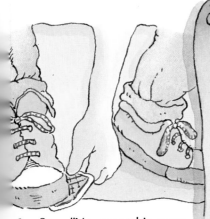

7 Try this script:
You: Tell me, is this the card you chose?
Friend: No!
You (looking worried): Oh dear, can I try again?
Take off your shoe, Ask your friend to take the piece of paper out and read the message. It correctly names their card: the 8 of Hearts. Everyone will be KNOCKED OUT!

6 Say: "Your card is now under my right foot." Pick up the card and show it.

Card words

These are some special words used in card magic

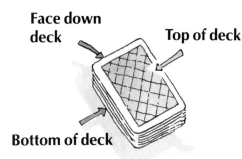

Face down deck

Top of deck

Bottom of deck

Face up deck

Face up card

Face down card

Shuffling

Shuffling

To shuffle is to change the order of all the cards in a deck. There are different ways to do this. You can hold the deck in one hand and lift up some cards with the other. Put the cards back into the deck, a few at a time in different places, so the order of the cards is changed. Repeat this until all the cards have changed places.

Cutting

Cutting

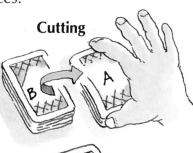

1 Cutting is a simple way of changing the order of cards in a deck. Take some of the cards (A) off the top of the deck and put them down to one side.

2 To complete the cut, pick up the bottom half of the deck (B) and put it on top of the rest (A).

Now have some fun with Money Magic...

Money Magic

All about money magic

This section shows you how to do thirteen great tricks with coins. On these pages you can find some tips and hints to help you become a successful magician.

You don't have to dress up to do tricks, but it's fun to wear a **cloak** and **hat** for special performances, and they may help you give a particularly brilliant performance!

Remember, **pockets** are very important pieces of equipment. Make sure your performing outfit has good-sized, easily reached pockets.

Some tricks require **special equipment** such as tape, scissors, rubber bands, etc. Where these things are needed they are listed at the beginning of each trick.

The most important thing your need is **practice.** Try tricks out over and over again in private until you can do them easily and smoothly.

Tricks are usually described and illustrated from the right-handed person's point of view. If you are left-handed just reverse the instructions. Perform tricks in whatever way feels most comfortable for you.

Try tricks out in front of a mirror so you can get an "audience's eye view."

Tricks with money are fun to do. As you learn how to do the tricks in this section, you will find out how to make money vanish, change in value, or even multiply itself! Everyone is interested in money, so it should be easy to hold your audience's attention.

Coins are not usually very clean, so don't put them near your mouth. Wash you hands after handling coins.

One special piece of equipment is a **coin chute.** You can learn how to make one on page 72.

Hints

1 Money tricks are most effective if you borrow the coins from your audience, rather than use your own. That way everyone will know you have not used special trick coins, and they will be even more impressed by your magic skills.

2 Make sure you have all the equipment ready and in the right place before you start to do a trick.

3 Keep your secrets secret! Don't show people how tricks work. And don't repeat tricks straight away, as someone may realize how the trick is done.

The drop flip

Things you need.

Any coin

Drop a coin on the floor, and make it vanish into thin air!

Trick time

This simple trick is suprisingly convincing when done well.

1 Show the coin to your audience. As you do so pretend to be clumsy and drop the coin on the floor near your foot.

2 While everyone laughs at you, bend down to pick up the coin, apologizing for your clumsiness.

3 Quickly flip the coin under your shoe with your fingertips.

4 Make a fist with your hand, as if you had picked up the coin, and stand up. Then open your hand – and the coin has vanished!

Strike a light!

Things you need

Any small coin   Matchbox

Make a coin disappear from a matchbox

Trick time

Practice this easy-to-learn trick until it works smoothly.

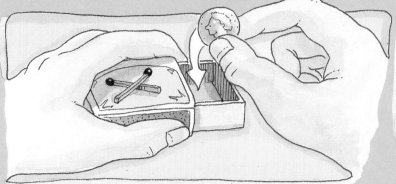

1 Show everyone that the matchbox is empty. Then ask someone to put a coin inside. Close the box and hold it between a finger and thumb, with your palm facing you.

2 Shake the box about so your friends can hear the coin rattling inside.

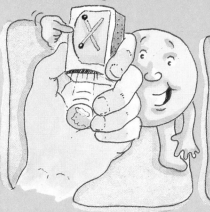

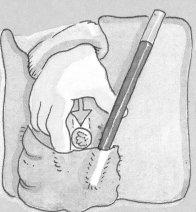

3 Squeeze the sides of the box so the top opens slightly. The coin will drop out into your palm.

4 Put the box on the table. Take the magic wand out of your pocket. At the same time drop the coin in!

5 Wave the wand over the box and ask someone to open it – and it's empty!

Hanky panky

Things you need

Small rubber band

Large handkerchief

Small piece of adhesive putty

Two easy ways to make a coin disappear under a handkerchief.

Trick time

Hanky panky **1**

1 Hide the rubber band in your right hand.

2 Drape the handkerchief over your hand. As you do so, slip your thumb and first and second fingers into the rubber band.

3 Borrow a coin from the audience and push it into the handkerchief. Make sure it goes into the circle made by your fingers stretching the rubber band.

4 Release your thumb and fingers and the rubber band will close, trapping the coin. Now you can shake the handkerchief – and the coin has vanished!

The coin is in this lump at the back!

Hanky panky

1   Hold the handkerchief out between your hands, with the adhesive putty hidden under your first finger.

2   Lay the handkerchief down on the table, pressing the adhesive putty onto it.

3   Ask someone to put a coin down on the middle of the handkerchief.

4   Pick up the corner with the adhesive putty on it and fold it over the coin, secretly pressing the putty down onto it.

5   Fold the other three corners into the center.

6   Take hold of the edges of the handkerchief and slide your hands apart until they are holding the corners.

7   Shake the handkerchief – and the coin has vanished!

Cheeky!

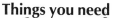

Things you need

Handful of coins

Jacket or pants
with pockets

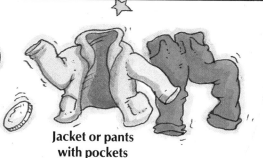

This trick is so simple
you'll need to be really
clever to get away
with it!

Get ready . . .

Start out with the coins in your right
pocket. Practice the following moves
carefully.

1 Take the coins out of
your pocket and hold them
in a pile in your right hand.

*keep the back of
your hand facing
toward your
audience.*

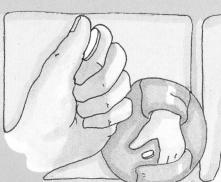

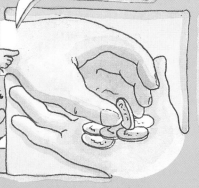

2 Reach across with your
left hand and pick out one
of the coins

3 Close your left hand into
a fist and **at the same time**
put all the other coins back
in your pocket.

4 Open your left hand and
show the coin.

56

Practice the four moves shown on the opposite page until you can perform them easily and smoothly. Now you can try the trick.

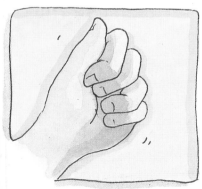

Trick time

1 When you perform this trick, do all four actions as before - but with one big difference — **don't actually take a coin!**

2 Hold the coins in your hand as before. But when you get to Stage 2, only **pretend** to take a coin.

So long as everyone **thinks** there's a coin in your left hand, you can make it seem to "disappear" in any way you like. Why not try inventing your own tricks?

3 Close your fist over an imaginary coin. Behave exactly as you did when there was a coin in it.

4 At the final stage, tap your left hand with your magic wand. Then open it and show there's nothing there!

57

Double your money

Things you need

Twelve small coins, all of the same value

Paper bag

Large hardback dictionary

Tip six coins into an empty bag – and take twelve coins out of it!

Get ready . . .

1 Open the dictionary at about the middle. You will now find a gap between the spine and the pages of the book.

Hide the coins in here.

2 Slide six of the coins into this space. When you close the book they should be held safely in place.

Trick time

1 Ask your friends what the word "magic" means. Say you will check it in your dictionary. Pick up the dictionary, open it near the middle and look for the word "magic."

2 Read out the definition and say you will now do some magic by making money double in value!

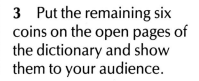

3 Put the remaining six coins on the open pages of the dictionary and show them to your audience.

Of course, the six coins from inside the binding also fall into the bag.

4 Open the paper bag, say some magic words, or wave your wand over it, and tip the coins into it.

5 Close the bag by twisting the paper around. Give the bag to one of your audience.

6 Ask your friend to open the bag and count the contents. To everyone's surprise the money has doubled in value!

The spooky pencil

Things you need

Small coin

Pencil

Piece of paper about 4 inches square

Push a pencil right through a coin wrapped in paper!

Get ready . . .

Make sure you are wearing something that has pockets. Put the pencil in your right-hand pocket.

Trick time

1 Lay the coin on the paper. Fold the paper as shown in drawings **a-d**, making a little package.

a Fold the bottom edge of the paper up to cover the coin.

b Fold the left side behind the coin.

c Fold the right side behind the coin.

Now the coin is in a little package. Only you know it's open at the top.

d Fold the flap down behind, *not* over the gap at the top.

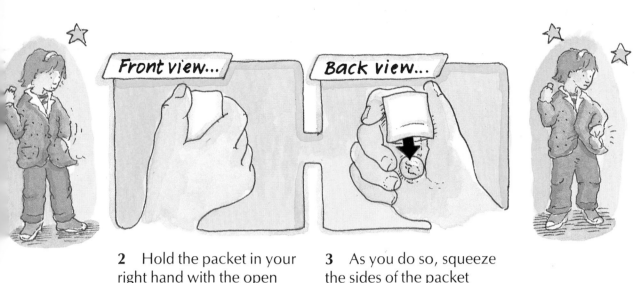

Front view... **Back view...**

2 Hold the packet in your right hand with the open edge **downward.** Put your left hand into your left pocket, looking for the pencil.

3 As you do so, squeeze the sides of the packet gently and the coin will fall into your palm.

4 Of course, you fail to find the pencil in your left pocket. So, transfer the paper packet to your left hand. Put your right hand into your right pocket, taking out the pencil and **dropping the coin in!**

5 Take the paper packet and push the pencil right through it. It looks as if you've pushed it right through the coin!

Drop the coin into your pocket. Then take the pencil out.

6 Pass the pencil and paper around for people to examine. Then tear the paper off the pencil - the coin has vanished!

The hypnotized coin

Things you need

Pin

Any large coin

Make a coin move as if hypnotized!

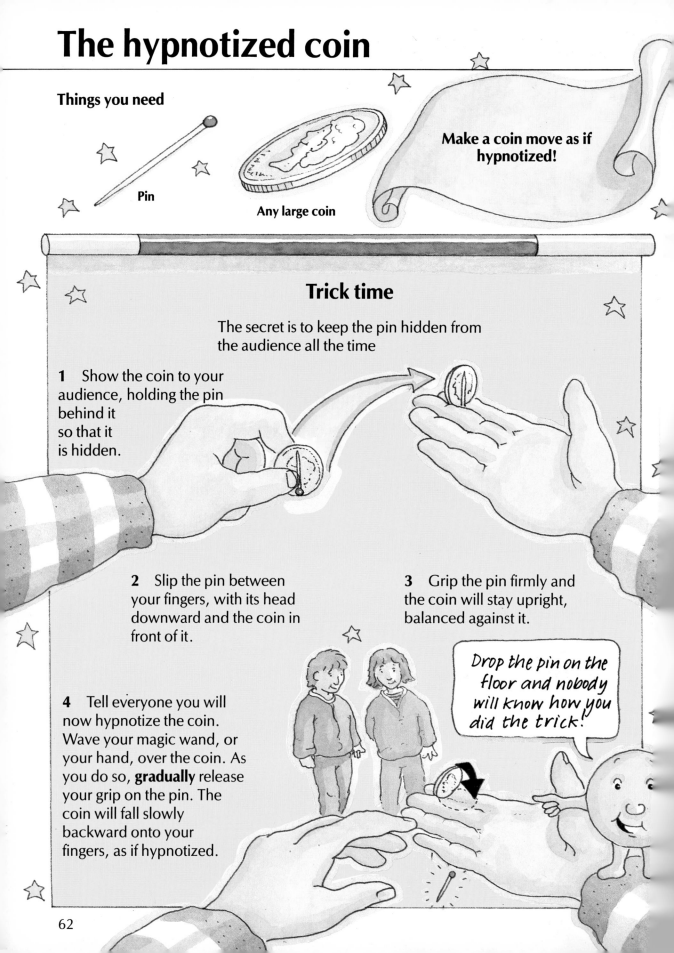

Trick time

The secret is to keep the pin hidden from the audience all the time

1 Show the coin to your audience, holding the pin behind it so that it is hidden.

2 Slip the pin between your fingers, with its head downward and the coin in front of it.

3 Grip the pin firmly and the coin will stay upright, balanced against it.

4 Tell everyone you will now hypnotize the coin. Wave your magic wand, or your hand, over the coin. As you do so, **gradually** release your grip on the pin. The coin will fall slowly backward onto your fingers, as if hypnotized.

Drop the pin on the floor and nobody will know how you did the trick!

The smashing grab

Things you need

Lots of practice!

Any coin

Make a coin disappear from your hands

Trick time

This way of making a coin vanish can be performed on its own or used as part of another trick. Practice your hand movements until they are absolutely smooth and convincing.

If you're left-handed you may find it easier to use the opposite hands.

1 Hold the coin in your left hand, gripping it between your thumb and first finger. Keep your palm cupped underneath.

2 Move your right hand toward the coin, putting your thumb behind the coin and fingers in front of it. Pretend to grab the coin, but when the fingers of the right hand are hiding it from your audience, **drop it into your left palm.**

Slowly open your right hand – and there's nothing in it!

3 Go on grabbing with your right hand, closing it into a fist and moving it away as if the coin were inside. Keep your left hand still, with the coin hidden in your palm, held there by the second and third fingers.

Empty

The coin is in here

Magic elbows

Things you need

Any coin

A shirt, blouse, or jacket with a collar

You will also need to be able to do *The smashing grab* trick shown on page 63.

Make a coin disappear by rubbing it on your elbow. Then rub the other elbow and make it reappear!

Trick time

Sit at a table to do this trick

The coin is in here

1 Hold the coin in your left hand, as if you were about to do the smashing grab trick (see page 63).

2 Move your right hand toward the coin. Then, instead of **pretending** to take the coin (as in the smashing grab) actually take it in your right hand.

3 Rest your head on your left hand and rub the coin against your left elbow with your fingers.

Oops!

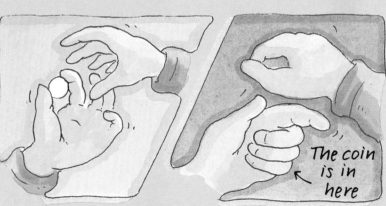

The coin is in here

4 Act clumsily and drop the coin onto the table with a clatter. Oh dear, you'd better try again!

5 Take the coin in your left hand as before, but this time do the smashing grab routine properly, so the coin remains hidden in your **left** hand.

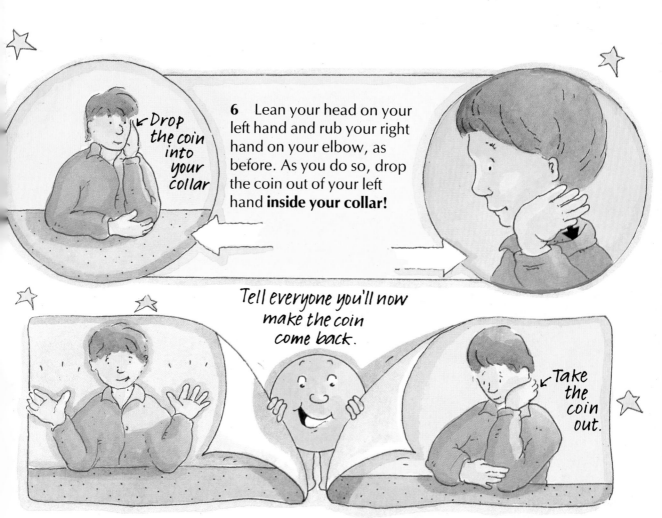

6 Lean your head on your left hand and rub your right hand on your elbow, as before. As you do so, drop the coin out of your left hand **inside your collar!**

Tell everyone you'll now make the coin come back.

7 After a few seconds, stop rubbing and show there's nothing in your right hand. The coin is rubbed away! Show there's nothing in your left hand, either.

8 Lean your head on your left hand and again rub your elbow with the other hand. **Grab the coin from your collar and hide it in your left hand.**

9 Rubbing your left elbow doesn't bring the coin back, so lean on the right hand and rub your **right** elbow with your left hand. (Of course the coin's now in your left hand.) After a few seconds, let the coin fall from your elbow onto the table. Your rubbing has made it come back!

Heads you lose

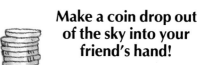 

Things you need

Any coin, preferably large

Make a coin drop out of the sky into your friend's hand!

Trick time

With practice this trick is very convincing – and baffling.

1 Stand facing a friend holding the coin in one hand. Ask the friend to hold out a hand toward you, palm up.

Say you will count up to three, and when you say "Three" they must try to grab the coin. If they can get it, they can keep it!

2 Raise your hand above your head, then bring the coin down onto their palm.

3 As you press you hand into their palm, call out "One!"

4 Raise your hand above your head again, bring down the coin onto their palm and count "Two!"

66

5 Raise your hand again, this time placing the coin **on the top of your head!**

6 Lower your hand, press it into their palm and call out "Three!" At the same moment your friend will make a grab for the coin.

7 Your friend now opens his or her hand - but there is no coin in it. Open your hand, too, and show the coin has vanished.

8 To make the coin come back, ask the friend to hold their hand out again and stare down at the palm, saying to themselves: "Magic money come back!"

Bend over slightly so the coin drops off the top of your head into their hand. Look up to the sky in amazement, as if you can hardly believe it yourself!

Tricky papers

Things you need

Ruler

Two squares of red paper about 4x4 inches

Two squares of white paper about 5x5 inches

Glue

Two squares of blue paper about 6x6 inches

Wrap a coin in three layers of paper – then make it disappear!

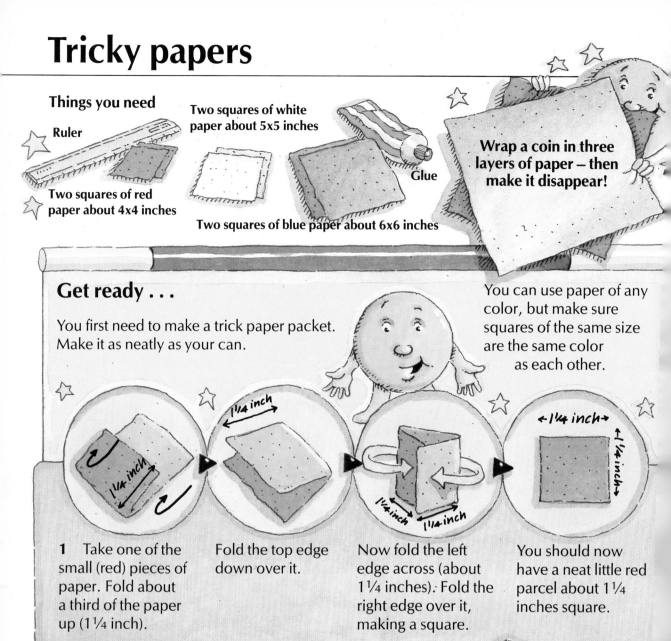

Get ready . . .

You first need to make a trick paper packet. Make it as neatly as your can.

You can use paper of any color, but make sure squares of the same size are the same color as each other.

1¼ inch

1¼ inch

1¼ inch

1¼ inch

←1¼ inch→

1¼ inch

1 Take one of the small (red) pieces of paper. Fold about a third of the paper up (1¼ inch).

Fold the top edge down over it.

Now fold the left edge across (about 1¼ inches). Fold the right edge over it, making a square.

You should now have a neat little red parcel about 1¼ inches square.

2 Place the red packet on the center of one of the pieces of white paper. Fold the white paper around it in the same way to make a packet about 1½ inches square.

3 Place the white packet on the center of one of the pieces of blue paper. Fold the blue paper around it in the same way to make a packet about 2 inches square.

68

4 Now make an **identical** set of packets with the other pieces of red, white, and blue paper. Make sure they are all the same size. **Stick the backs of the blue packets together to make a double packet.**

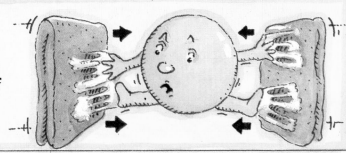

Trick time

1 Place your trick paper packets on the table and open the top set of papers so it looks like this:

2 Borrow a coin from your audience. Put it at the center of the red paper and fold the red packet up.

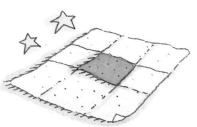

3 Put the red packet on the white paper and fold the sides to make a packet.

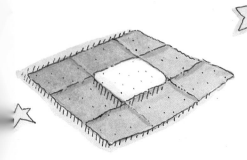

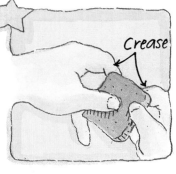

Crease

4 Put the white packet on the blue paper and fold the blue paper around it.

5 Pick up the blue packet when you fold it, carefully creasing the edges. As you do so, **turn the packet over** so the second set of packets (with no coin inside) is on top. Do this casually and nobody will notice.

6 Put the packet back on the table, empty side on top. Wave your magic wand, or your hand, over it. Open the blue packet and take out the white. Then open the white packet and take out the red. Give the red packet to a member of the audience to open.

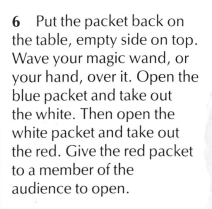

Surprise, surprise! There's nothing in it!

The amazing sealed boxes

Things you need

Two matchboxes, one fitting inside the other

Small piece of cloth

Nine rubber bands

Coin chute (see page 72)

Small coin

Scissors

Needle and thread

Make a marked coin appear by magic inside a sealed bag, inside *two* sealed boxes!

Get ready . . .

1 Fold the cloth and sew it to make a tiny bag. Make sure the end of the coin chute will fit into it.

Turn the bag inside out.

2 Make sure the equipment is the right size.

The end of the chute must fit inside the smaller matchbox.

The small coin must drop easily through the chute.

3 Put one end of the chute into the cloth bag. Fasten with a rubber band.

The small matchbox must fit inside the large one.

4 Put the chute and bag into the small matchbox. Fasten four rubber bands around the box.

5 Put the small matchbox inside the large one, with the chute poking out at one end. Put four rubber bands around the larger box, two in each direction.

Put the boxes and the chute in your left pocket.

Trick time

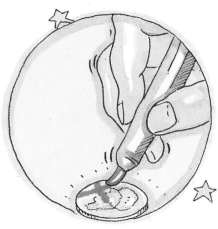

1 Ask the audience for a small coin (of the same size as one you know goes easily through the chute.)

2 Ask the person who gives it to you to mark the coin with a pen so they will recognize it again.

See page 63.

3 Do a "smashing grab" coin vanish (see page 63) so everyone thinks the coin's in your right hand . . . but it's in your *left* hand. Put your left hand into your pocket and drop the coin into the end of the chute.

4 Pull the chute out of the matchboxes. Leave the chute in your pocket and take the boxes out.

5 Give the boxes to a member of the audience. Slowly open your right hand – and the coin has gone!

All the rubber bands have tightened, so the boxes are sealed.

That's fantastic!

6 Ask the person to open the sealed matchbox. There's another sealed box inside, with a little bag in it. And inside **that** is the marked coin!

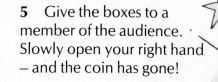

Make a coin chute

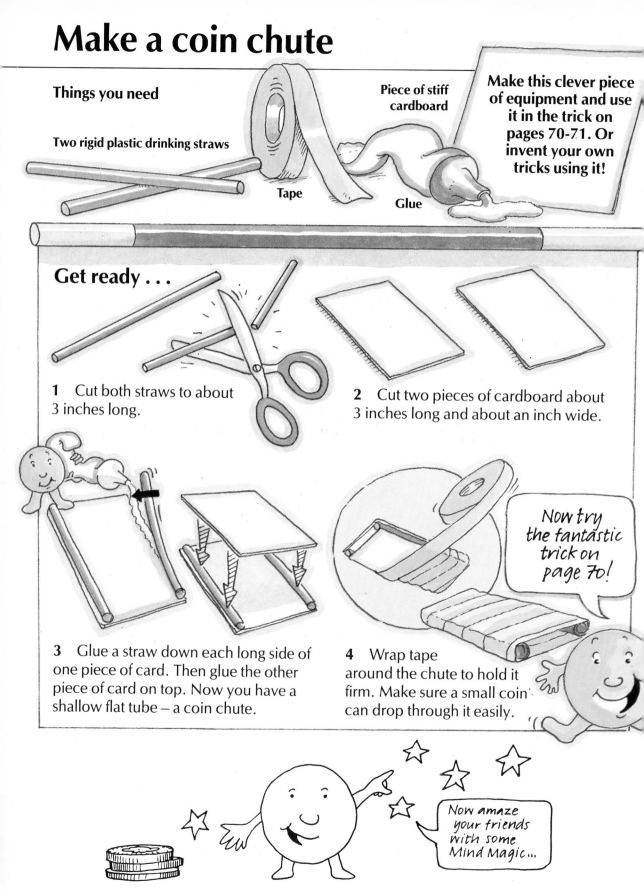

Things you need

Two rigid plastic drinking straws

Piece of stiff cardboard

Tape

Glue

Make this clever piece of equipment and use it in the trick on pages 70-71. Or invent your own tricks using it!

Get ready . . .

1 Cut both straws to about 3 inches long.

2 Cut two pieces of cardboard about 3 inches long and about an inch wide.

3 Glue a straw down each long side of one piece of card. Then glue the other piece of card on top. Now you have a shallow flat tube – a coin chute.

4 Wrap tape around the chute to hold it firm. Make sure a small coin can drop through it easily.

Now try the fantastic trick on page 70!

Now amaze your friends with some Mind Magic...

Mind Magic

All about mind magic

This section shows you ten different ways to convince your friends that you can read their minds! Here are some tips to help you do this successfully.

Mind magic is difficult to do because you have to persuade people to believe you. Your audience must see what you want them to see and think what you want them to think! Try to make your **presentation** as dramatic as possible. It is not enough just to learn how the "trick" works.

You don't have to dress up, but wearing a **cloak** and **hat** is fun and may help you give a better performance.

Two important things you need to be a good magician are **practice** and **acting ability**.

IMPORTANT

When doing mind magic, be careful not to use the word "trick." Mind magicians prefer the word "**experiments.**" If you call what you are doing an experiment, the audience is much more likely to think you really *can* read their minds and are not tricking them!

For some mindreading experiments you will need pencils, books, paper, scissors, etc. There is a list of these things at the beginning of each "trick."

Hints

1 When you are performing mind magic, it is much more convincing if you are not absolutely right all the time. Have a "near miss" sometimes. For example, if you are trying to find out someone's name by mindreading, and you know the name is Suzie, you could try "Susan" or "Sue."

2 Don't explain to anyone how you do your experiments. Keep your secrets secret!

3 Don't repeat experiments straight away, even if people in the audience ask you to do so. Someone may see how the experiment was done!

4 At the beginning of each experiment, make sure you've got all the equipment ready and in the right place.

The mystery calculator

Things you need

Copies of the number cards given below

Read your friends' minds so you know what number they are thinking of.

Get ready . . .

You will need to make copies of the seven mystery calculator cards shown here. Photocopy them, color them, cut them out and past them onto cardboard.

1	3	5	7	9	11	13	15
17	19	21	23	25	27	29	31
33	35	37	39	41	43	45	47
49	51	53	55	57	59	61	63
65	67	69	71	73	75	77	79
81	83	85	87	89	91	93	95
97	99						

2	3	6	7	10	11	14	15
18	19	22	23	26	27	30	31
34	35	38	39	42	43	46	47
50	51	54	55	58	59	62	63
66	67	70	71	74	75	78	79
82	83	86	87	90	91	94	95
98	99						

4	5	6	7	12	13	14	15
20	21	22	23	28	29	30	31
36	37	38	39	44	45	46	47
52	53	54	55	60	61	62	63
68	69	70	71	76	77	78	79
84	85						

8	9	10	11	12	13	14	15
24	25	26	27	28	29	30	31
40	41	42	43	44	45	46	47
56	57	58	59	60	61	62	63
72	73	74	75	76	77	78	79
88	89	90	91	92	93	94	95

16	17	18	19	20	21	22	23
24	25	26	27	28	29	30	31
48	49	50	51	52	53	54	55
56	57	58	59	60	61	62	63
80	81	82	83	84	85	86	87
88	89	90	91	92	93	94	95

32	33	34	35	36	37	38	39
40	41	42	43	44	45	46	47
48	49	50	51	52	53	54	55
56	57	58	59	60	61	62	63
96	97	98	99				

64	65	66	67	68	69	70	71
72	73	74	75	76	77	78	79
80	81	82	83	84	85	86	87
88	89	90	91	92	93	94	95
96	97	98	99				

Trick time

1 Ask a friend to think of any number between one and 100. Tell them to keep the number secret.

2 When they are ready, check they don't want to change the number. Let them do so, if they wish.

Think of a number

23

3 Tell them to concentrate on their chosen number. Now give them the seven mystery calculator cards.

4 Ask them to look at the cards and give you back **every card that has their chosen number on it.**

5 As soon as they have done this, you can tell exactly what number they chose!

If you find it hard to believe, try the mystery calculator yourself!

2

4

16

How? The answer's easy: just add together the numbers in the top left-hand corner of the cards your friend gives you.

For example, if they chose the number 23, they will hand you the blue, yellow, pink, and white cards. The numbers in the top left-hand corners are 1 + 2 + 4 + 16 – and these add up to 23!

23

Who's who?

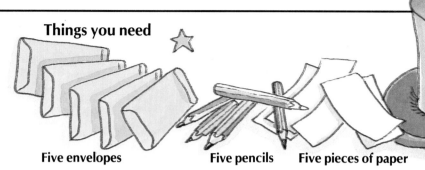

Things you need

Five envelopes   Five pencils   Five pieces of paper

> Look inside your friends' minds and find out who they would like to be.

Get ready . . .

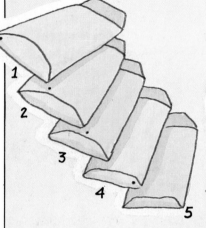

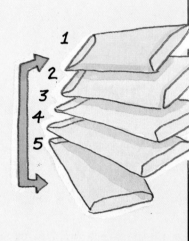

1 Use a pencil to mark four of the envelopes with dots. Put the dots in different places, as shown here. Leave the fifth envelope blank.

2 Now you can tell which envelope is which by looking at the dots. Put them in a pile with envelope number 1 on top.

Trick time

They can disguise their handwriting as much as they like!

1 Ask your friends to sit in a row. Give each one a pencil, a piece of paper, and an envelope. Give out the envelopes in order, so number 1 goes to the friend in position 1, and so on.

2 Now tell your friends to write down the name of someone they would really like to be.

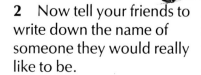

3 When they've finished, tell them to fold up the paper and put it into the envelope.

4 Collect up the envelopes (or get an assistant to do so). Thoroughly mix up the envelopes on the table.

5 Pick up one envelope secretly looking for your pencil mark to find out which person it belongs to.

6 Open the envelope and look at the name on the paper. But don't give the game away too soon. Read out the name for example "Queen Elizabeth 1," and say: "I wonder who wants to be Queen Elizabeth 1?"

7 Study your friends carefully for a few moments. Then put your hand on the right person's shoulder and say: "YOU want to be Queen Elizabeth!" Repeat this with the next envelope. Everyone will be amazed!

8 Now there are three minds left to read. Open another envelope and read the name out. For example, imagine the name is Napoleon. Tell the three remaining friends that you will ask each of them if they want to be Napolean. They must all answer "No." You will be able to tell who's lying and who's telling the truth!

9 Finally, open the last two envelopes, noting which people they belong to. Read both names out, think hard, then give the correct piece of paper to each person!

The right touch

Things you need

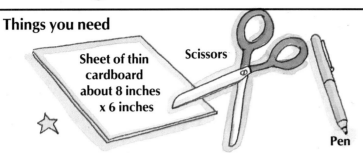

Sheet of thin cardboard about 8 inches x 6 inches

Scissors

Pen

Control your friend's mind so he or she is forced to touch the card you choose!

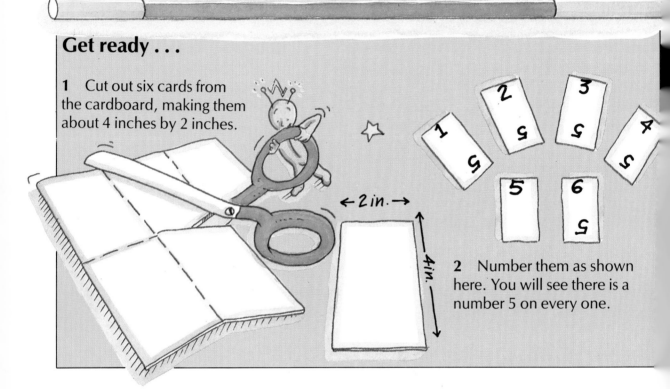

Get ready . . .

1 Cut out six cards from the cardboard, making them about 4 inches by 2 inches.

←2 in.→

4 in.

2 Number them as shown here. You will see there is a number 5 on every one.

1 Hold the cards in a fan shape in your hand. Make sure your thumb covers the figure 5 on the top card.

2 Tell your friend you can control his or her mind so that you make them touch card number 5! As you say this, close up the fan **from left to right.**

3 Take the cards in your right hand, **turning them as your do so.** Now the figure 5s are on the top edge.

4 Shuffle the cards and fan them with the backs facing your audience.

5 Hold the fan up and ask your friend to touch the back of one of the cards.

6 Take the chosen card out carefully, holding your thumb over the number at the bottom.

7 Turn the card over - and your friend *has* chosen the number 5 card! There's a 1 in 5 chance they'll choose the real number 5 card anyway, so you can't lose!

What's the score?

Roll dice inside a matchbox and guess which numbers will be showing when you open it up!

Things you need

Four small dice

Matchbox

Glue

Small piece of paper

Pencil

Get ready . . .

1 Make sure the matchbox is big enough for the dice to roll about inside.

2 Glue two dice to one end of the floor of the matchbox. Glue them to show any combination of numbers. This example shows a 6 and a 3. Remember what numbers you choose!

3 Mark the lid of the box with a pencil dot so you can tell which is the empty end.

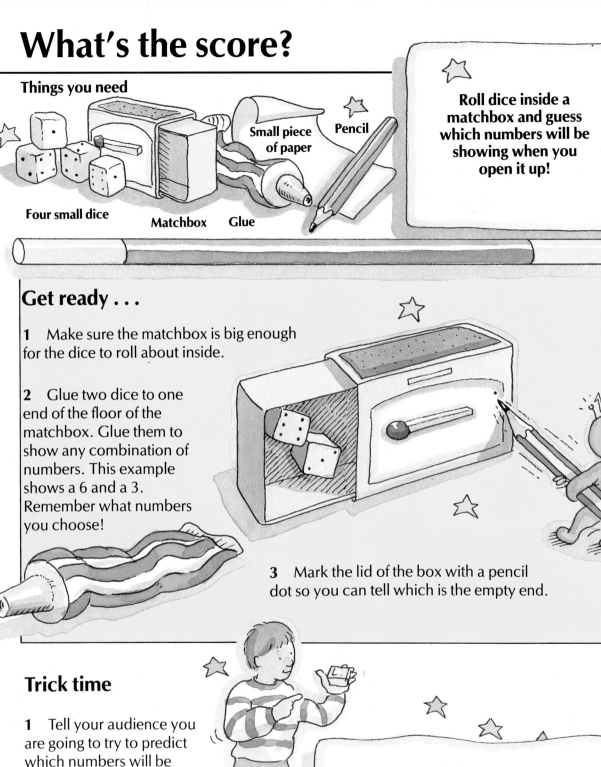

Trick time

1 Tell your audience you are going to try to predict which numbers will be showing on two dice after they have been shaken inside the matchbox.

2 Write your prediction on a piece of paper, not letting anyone see what you write. Put "I think the dice will total 9, made up of a 6 and a 3" (or whatever numbers you have chosen). Fold up the paper and give it to one of your audience. If they have a pocket, tuck the paper into it.

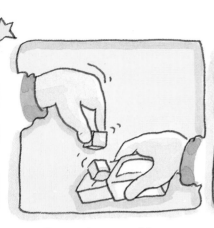

3   Open the matchbox **at the empty end** (the pencil dot end) and drop in the other two dice.

4   To show there is no trickery (!) shake the box, open it and show the two loose dice.

5   Tip the dice out. Ask a member of the audience to examine the dice, put them back into the box and then shake it up.

6   Take the box back and shake it again. Open it at the **other** (glued dice) end. Of course, the dice show a 6 and a 3.

I think the dice will total 9, made up of a 6 and a 3.

7   Ask the person to open your written prediction, which you made before the experiment began. And it is absolutely accurate!

8   If you like, you can make other boxes containing other combinations of dice. But make sure you know which box is which!

Your choice, my choice!

Things you need

Two complete decks of cards

Read your friend's mind so you both choose the same card!

Trick time

1 Try this experiment with a friend. Explain that they must do exactly what you do throughout.

This is the key card

2 Put both decks of cards on the table. Pick up one of them and ask your friend to pick up the other.

3 Shuffle your deck and ask your friend to shuffle theirs.

4 Here's the important bit: take a secret peep at the card on the bottom of your deck. Remember it.

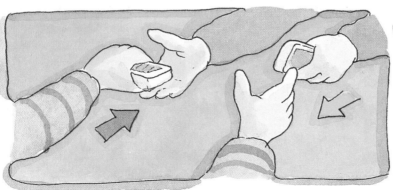

5 Swap decks of cards, so you take your friend's and he or she takes yours. Both decks have been shuffled, so nobody can know where any card is . . . right?

6 Spread your deck out, then remove any one card. Do not show it to anybody.

7 Ask your friend to spread out his or her deck and take out any one card in the same way.

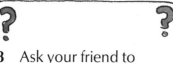

8 Ask your friend to remember which card they picked out. You need only *pretend* to remember your chosen card, but **do** remember the key card!

Gather your cards together and put your chosen card back on top. Ask your friend to put his or her card back on top of *their* deck.

9 Both of you now cut your decks (see above), so your chosen card moves to near the middle of the deck.

key card   Friend's chosen card

10 Your friend's chosen card is now **directly under the key card.**

11 Swap decks again. Fan the cards out from left to right and look through your friend's deck while they look through yours. Your friend should look for his or her chosen card. You look for the key card.

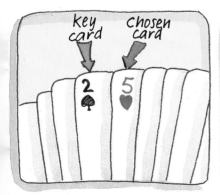

key card   chosen card

2♠   5♥

12 The card on the right of the key card is the one your friend chose. Put it face down on the table.

13 Ask your friend to put his or her chosen card next to it, face down. Ask if they believe in coincidences!

The same!

14 Turn over the two cards . . . and they are the same! What a coincidence!

Pieces of eight . . .

Things you need

Eight small objects and a box to put them in.

For example:
Key, ring, match, button, battery, bracelet, safety pin, chewing gum.

Look into your friend's mind and see which object he or she is thinking about

Get ready . . .

1 Look at the list of objects you need: each one has a different number of letters in its name, from 3 letters (key) to 10 (chewing gum). You can subsitute other items, but make sure they have the right number of letters.

2 Make sure the objects are small enough for each to be hidden in a clenched hand.

3 Remember how many letters there are in the name of each object!

Object	Number of letters
KEY	3
RING	4
MATCH	5
BUTTON	6
BATTERY	7
BRACELET	8
SAFETY PIN	9
CHEWING GUM	10

You can use any objects with the right number of letters in the name.

Trick time

1 Put all 8 items on the table, with the box. Pick up the objects, in any order, one by one and put them in the box. As you do so, name each one out loud e.g. "Match," "Bracelet" etc.

2 Ask your friend to look into the box, choose one of the objects, and think about it.

3 Explain you will now lift the objects out of the box, one at a time. Each time you take an object out, your friend must spell out **one** letter of the name of their chosen object (in their head, silently). When they reach the last letter they must shout out "Stop!"

Keep the object hidden in your hand.

4 Put your hand into the box and take out any object, hidden in your clenched hand.

5 Wait a few seconds, then put your hand back into the box, drop the object in and take out another.

6 Put your hand in the box for the **third** time and take out the key. If your friend is thinking of the key (3 letters) he or she will shout "Stop!" You open your hand – and there is the key!

Stop!

That's fantastic!

7 If not, carry on. Take out the ring (4 letters). If they are thinking of the ring they will shout "Stop!" – and there is the ring in your hand!

8 Carry on taking out the objects with the next largest number of letters – until your friend shouts "Stop!" Whenever your open your hand the correct object will be in it!

Mind over money!

Things you need

Four coins of different values

Envelope

Pieces of cardboard a bit smaller than the envelope

Glue

Paper to make labels

Pen

Predict which of four coins your friend will choose . . . and be right every time.

Get ready . . .

1 On the front of the envelope write this message: "You will think of the quarter."

2 On one side of the card write "You will think of the dime."

3 Make a small label, write on it "You will think of this coin" and stick it on the cent.

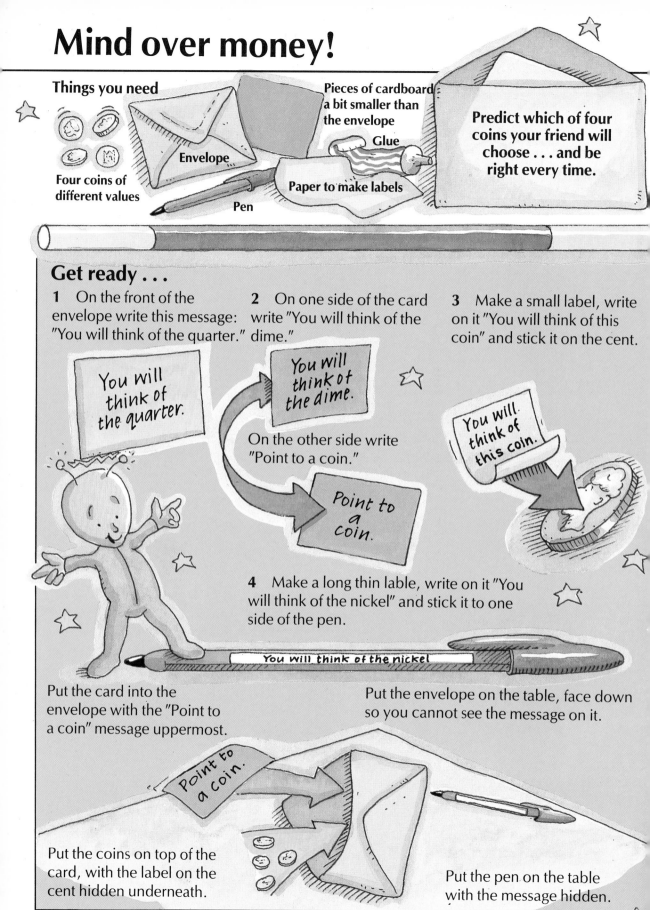

You will think of the quarter.

You will think of the dime.

On the other side write "Point to a coin."

Point to a coin.

You will think of this coin.

4 Make a long thin lable, write on it "You will think of the nickel" and stick it to one side of the pen.

You will think of the nickel

Put the card into the envelope with the "Point to a coin" message uppermost.

Put the envelope on the table, face down so you cannot see the message on it.

Point to a coin.

Put the coins on top of the card, with the label on the cent hidden underneath.

Put the pen on the table with the message hidden.

Trick time

1 Slide the card out of the envelope and put it on the table with "Point to a coin" message showing.

2 Slide the coins out of the envelope carefully and put them on the card.

3 Pick up the pen and point to the coins. Say:

In a moment I want you to choose one of these coins and then point to it ...

... but I already know which one you'll choose. I'm thinking about that coin and I'm sending your mind a message to make you choose the same one.

There are four endings to this trick, and they are all astonishing!

If they choose the dime slide the coins aside and ask them to turn over the card!

If they choose the cent ask them to turn over the other coins – and then the cent!

If they choose the quarter ask them to turn the envelope over!

If they choose the nickel give them the pen to write with while you put the coins back into the envelope and hide all the evidence away!

Magic clock

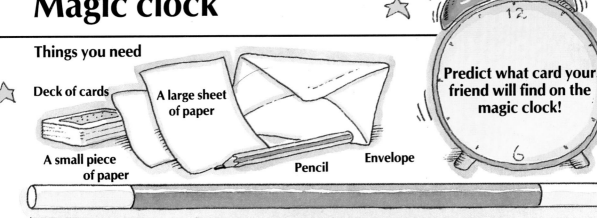

Things you need

Deck of cards

A small piece of paper

A large sheet of paper

Pencil

Envelope

Predict what card your friend will find on the magic clock!

Get ready . . .

This is a brilliant trick. Memorize all the moves carefully and it will always astonish everyone.

This is the 7 of Clubs.

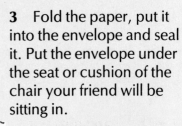

1 Choose any card from the deck. (Let's pretend it's the 7 of Clubs.) Put it back into the deck so it's the **thirteenth** card from the top. This is the card you will "predict."

2 On a small piece of paper write "You will pick up the 7 of Clubs."

3 Fold the paper, put it into the envelope and seal it. Put the envelope under the seat or cushion of the chair your friend will be sitting in.

4 Put the large sheet of paper, the pen, and the cards ready on the table.

Trick time

1 Ask a friend to sit on the chair where the note is hidden. Put the cards on the table in front of him or her, face down.

2 Draw a large circle on the paper and write the numbers 1 to 12 around the edges, like a clock face.

3   Ask your friend to think of any number from 1 to 12, and to keep it secret.

4   Turn your back on your friend and say: "Take the same number of cards off the top of the deck as the number you're thinking of, and then sit on them!"

For example, if they are thinking of the number 3, they take three cards off the top of the deck – and sit on them!

12 cards from the top of the deck.

The card by the 3.

5   Turn back and deal out the top 12 cards from the deck, one on top of the other, **so their order is reversed.**

6   Pick up these 12 cards and deal one to each number on the clock, **starting at 1 and ending at 12.**

7   Ask your friend to look at the clock and pick up the card that has been dealt to the number they chose.

8   Say you wrote a note before the trick began. Your friend is sitting on it. Ask them to look. All they will find are the cards they put there before. Apologize, take the cards, and ask your friend to look under the seat (or cushion) to find the note.

9   When they open the note it correctly predicts that they will pick up the 7 of Clubs. What a shock! Make sure your friend doesn't faint . . .

One in a million

Things you need

Deck of cards

Pencil

Large book

Piece of paper

Handkerchief or cloth

Read someone's mind and discover which word they chose from a book containing thousands of words!

Get ready . . .

The secret of this astonishing trick is that **you** first decide which word you want your friend to choose!

This is the magic word. Remember it!

Page 94

line 3

Word 7

1 Take any four number cards (not Kings, Queens, Jacks, or Aces) from your deck.

2 If you have chosen, for example, a 9, a 4, a 3, and a 7, think of this as three numbers: 94, 3 and 7. Turn to page 94 in your book. Look at line 3 (third from the top) and find the 7th word on it.

3 Put the four chosen cards back on top of the pack so the 9 is on top, 4 is in second place, 3 is in third place, and the 7 is in fourth place.

9 4 3 7

Trick time

1 Hand the book to your friend and say you want him or her to choose a word from it using a random selection of cards.

This is the tricky bit!

2 Place the cards **face down** on your left palm. Cover your hand and the deck with the handkerchief.

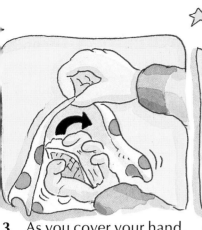

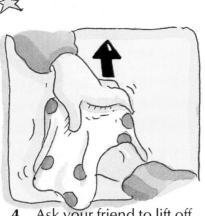

3 As you cover your hand, flip the deck over so it is now **face up.** Practice until you can do it smoothly.

4 Ask your friend to lift off the top part of the deck, through the handkerchief.

5 Secretly flip the cards in your hand **face down** again as you take the handkerchief and other cards from your friend.

6 Ask your friend to take the top two cards off the deck in your hand (the 9 and the 4). They make the page number. Tell them to find page 94 in the book.

7 The next card (the 3) gives them the line number. The next one (the 7) gives the number of the word on that line.

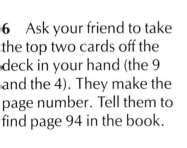

Well, you knew the word all along, so it shouldn't be difficult.

8 Ask your friend to find the word and think hard about it because you are going to read his or her mind.

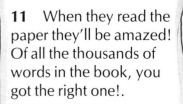

9 Act like mad, looking as if you're concentrating hard. Write down the word on the piece of paper.

10 Fold the paper up and give it to your friend. Ask them to tell you what the chosen word was and then to read out the word on the paper.

11 When they read the paper they'll be amazed! Of all the thousands of words in the book, you got the right one!.

Name that card

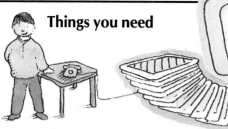

Things you need

An assistant with a telephone

Deck of cards

Two copies of the coded list, given below

Mindreading over the telephone . . . that's not possible is it? Oh yes it is . . .

Get ready . . .

1 Make two copies of the lists given here. Give one to the assistant. Keep one for yourself. Write your assistant's phone number at the top.

2 Arrange for your assistant to be at home when you do this stunning "experiment!"

Change the names if you like, but use each name only once.

Use the girls' list if your assistant is a girl.

If your assistant is a boy, use the boys' name list.

TELEPHONE NUMBER...

	HEARTS	SPADES	DIAMONDS	CLUBS
Ace	Abigail	Alexandra	Alison	Amanda
2	Barbara	Carol	Caroline	Catherine
3	Christine	Claire	Danielle	Dawn
4	Debbie	Denise	Dianne	Donna
5	Elaine	Elizabeth	Emily	Emma
6	Fiona	Helen	Isobel	Janet
7	Jean	Jenny	Jill	Joanne
8	Julie	Karen	Katie	Laura
9	Linda	Lisa	Lorraine	Lucy
10	Mandy	Mary	Melanie	Michelle
Jack	Natalie	Nicola	Paula	Philippa
Queen	Rachel	Rebecca	Ruth	Sally
King	Samantha	Sarah	Sharon	Suzy
Joker: Victoria				

TELEPHONE NUMBER...

	HEARTS	SPADES	DIAMONDS	CLUBS
Ace	Adam	Alexander	Andrew	Anthony
2	Ben	Charles	Christopher	Daniel
3	David	Dean	Donald	Douglas
4	Edward	Frank	Gary	Gavin
5	Graham	Harry	Harvey	Howard
6	Hugh	Ian	Ivor	Jack
7	James	Jason	Joe	Jonathan
8	Justin	Kevin	Luke	Mark
9	Martin	Matthew	Michael	Nathan
10	Nicholas	Oliver	Patrick	Paul
Jack	Peter	Philip	Richard	Robert
Queen	Rupert	Russell	Ryan	Simon
King	Stewart	Tim	Tom	Victor
Joker: William				